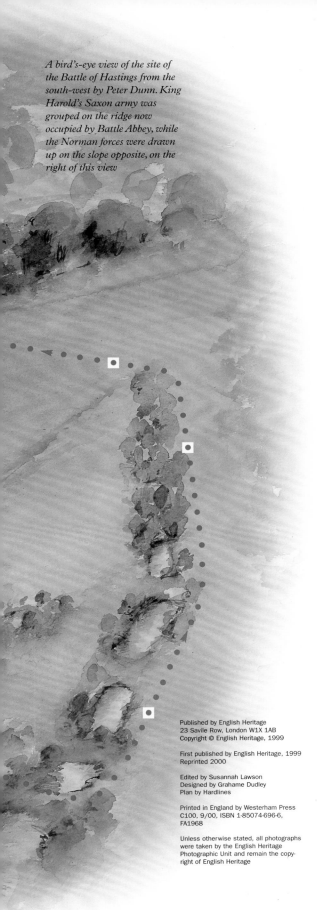

*A bird's-eye view of the site of the Battle of Hastings from the south-west by Peter Dunn. King Harold's Saxon army was grouped on the ridge now occupied by Battle Abbey, while the Norman forces were drawn up on the slope opposite, on the right of this view*

Published by English Heritage
23 Savile Row, London W1X 1AB
Copyright © English Heritage, 1999

First published by English Heritage, 1999
Reprinted 2000

Edited by Susannah Lawson
Designed by Grahame Dudley
Plan by Hardlines

Printed in England by Westerham Press
C100, 9/00, ISBN 1-85074-696-6,
FA1968

Unless otherwise stated, all photographs were taken by the English Heritage Photographic Unit and remain the copyright of English Heritage

# THE BATTLE OF HASTINGS

## AND THE STORY OF BATTLE ABBEY

TEXT ON BATTLE ABBEY BY JONATHAN COAD, MA, FSA

TEXT ON THE BATTLE OF HASTINGS BY ANDREW BOXER

# CONTENTS

The Battle of Hastings, fought here on 14 October 1066, is one of the most famous battles in history, when Harold of England and William of Normandy contested the English throne. It was the last successful hostile invasion of England, heralding the establishment of a new ruling élite, and the transformation of Anglo-Saxon society. Battle Abbey was founded soon after by King William, out of gratitude for his victory. This guidebook begins with a tour of the abbey buildings and the battlefield, followed by a detailed account of the battle and a history of the abbey.

Jonathan Coad is an Inspector of Ancient Monuments for the South-East region of English Heritage. Andrew Boxer is Head of the History Department and Director of Studies at Eastbourne College, East Sussex.

# Tour of the Battlefield and Abbey

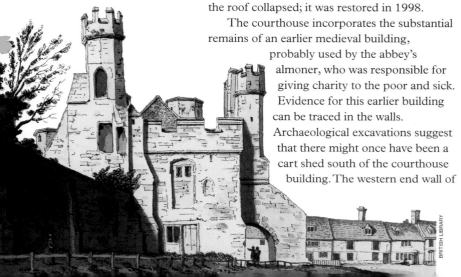

*Engraving of the abbey gatehouse early in the nineteenth century (detail)*

BRITISH LIBRARY

~ THE GREAT GATEHOUSE IS ONE OF THE FINEST MONASTIC GATEHOUSES IN ENGLAND ~

*A view of the east end of the sixteenth-century courthouse showing the remains of a medieval building incorporated in the courthouse. Beyond lies the abbey gatehouse.*

## THE COURTHOUSE

*The tour starts at the shop, housed in the former courthouse of the abbey. Walk through the shop and stop on the path just outside.*

The building which now houses the shop was once the courthouse. It dates largely from the mid-sixteenth century when it was built to replace an earlier courthouse at the corner of Mount Street and the High Street. Courts were held on the first floor while the ground floor was used as a covered market. The building was abandoned in the late eighteenth century when the roof collapsed; it was restored in 1998.

The courthouse incorporates the substantial remains of an earlier medieval building, probably used by the abbey's almoner, who was responsible for giving charity to the poor and sick. Evidence for this earlier building can be traced in the walls. Archaeological excavations suggest that there might once have been a cart shed south of the courthouse building. The western end wall of this building can still be seen by the south-eastern turret of the gatehouse.

*Walk along the path until you are standing just by the gatehouse.*

## THE GREAT GATEHOUSE

The great gatehouse, one of the finest monastic gatehouses in England, linked the abbey to the outside world. Immediately inside lay the outer court with its barns, workshops, bakery and brewhouse and administrative offices. Through the gatehouse came tradesmen and merchants, local people wishing to worship in the nave of the abbey church, as well as important visitors for the abbot. The present structure dates largely from 1338, when the gatehouse was remodelled to provide a more magnificent entrance to the abbey and to increase security at a time of growing instability.

Substantial traces of the late eleventh- and twelfth-century structure incorporated in the range west of the gatehouse (to the left of the entrance), suggest that the earlier gateway lay a little to the west of the present entrance. Until 1538, the ground floor here would have provided accommodation for the abbey porter.

BRITISH LIBRARY

After the Dissolution in the 1530s (when Henry VIII disbanded all monastic houses) it had a variety of uses, including housing a malting kiln.

The gatehouse has prominent octagonal turrets at each corner. Those on the outer court side contain stairs to the upper floors. The stone porch on the south-eastern turret (on the right) was not part of the original design but was added soon afterwards, probably to emphasise the importance of the room to which it led. The gatehouse has two vaulted entrance passages; the smaller one for pedestrians, the larger one for wagons and horses.

The gatehouse is elaborately decorated on the outside – a symbol of the abbey's wealth. At first-floor level a rich band of decorative arcading extends round the corner turrets, while above are twin niches which probably once contained statues of saints. The gatehouse has several defensive features. On the second floor, the turrets have arrow loops rather than windows; and there are crenellated parapets above. The building is further enriched by a wealth of sculpture, notably on the vaulting inside the gate-passages. Human and animal heads, mythical beasts and foliage can all be seen. Much of this detail is original, but some has been renewed.

Originally, the upper floors of the gatehouse and the west wing provided spacious lodgings, that would have been used by important visitors if the abbot's guest range was full, or more likely by senior officials of the abbey – the beadle, collector of the abbey rents and revenues, or the steward. From around 1200 to 1330, the

steward, responsible for the legal aspects of the community's life, including the administration of justice in the land immediately surrounding the monastery, was invariably a legally trained monk. However, from the 1330s, Battle Abbey retained the services of lay stewards who came mostly from the gentry of Kent or Sussex and were just beginning their careers in law and administration. For such officials, the gatehouse apartments would have provided appropriately comfortable accommodation.

*Go through the porch in the south-eastern turret (on the right) and up the stairs. Look up at the ceiling when you reach the first window on the stairs.*

*The abbey gatehouse of 1338 from the south-west. This is one of the finest monastic gatehouses in England*

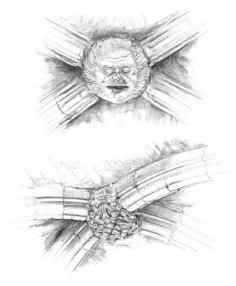

*Drawings of the fourteenth-century carved stone bosses in the vaults of the abbey gatehouse, by Peter Dunn*

Half-way up the stairs is a stern reminder of the troubled times when this gatehouse was being built. Here the archway over the stairs contains a portcullis groove and in front of it the vault has two murder-holes for defenders to rain down missiles on intruders below. Simple defences like arrow slits are not unknown in monastic gatehouses, but rarely were defences carried to this degree of sophistication. In effect, Battle Abbey gatehouse could become a miniature keep, unable to withstand a siege but certainly capable of resisting the sort of French raids which plagued coastal areas of eastern Sussex for much of the fourteenth century.

*Carry on up the stairs and into the great chamber, where there is an exhibition on the history of the site.*

On the left a doorway leads to the portcullis room. Originally, the great chamber would have been simply furnished, probably with a bed, a table, a chest and some benches and chairs near the fireplace. In the west wall of the great chamber is a modern copy of the huge medieval fire hood (based on evidence found during conservation work in 1988), which helps demonstrate something of the former appearance of this fourteenth-century room. At opposite ends of the north wall, doorways lead

*The medieval fireplace in the great chamber of the gatehouse. This is an accurate reconstruction based on fragments of the original discovered during conservation work in the 1980s*

to the northern turrets. These once had floors on each level and might have been used as cupboards.

*Walk through the door into the next room, which leads to the first floor of the west wing.*

Originally this was a separate lodging, approached by the spiral stairs in the south-west turret. The doorway from the great chamber is a later alteration. You can get a good view of the town from the far windows. Although now one room, it is possible that the north-eastern part might have been partitioned off as a separate bedchamber, lit by the single-light window in the north wall. In the west wall is a wall cupboard and a handsome stone fireplace. To the right of the fireplace is a blocked Norman window, belonging to the earlier building here. In the south-west corner (to the left of the fireplace) a narrow doorway leads to a vaulted two-cell garderobe or latrine tower.

*When you have finished looking round the exhibition, go down the stairs and stop just outside the gatehouse.*

## THE WEST RANGE

South of the gatehouse, across the former great court, stands the west range of the abbey – one of the best-preserved monastic west ranges in the country. This is now a school and is not open to visitors, except for the great hall during the summer holidays.

In a Benedictine abbey the west range was conventionally used by the cellarer for storing provisions. On the ground floor, next to the west end of the church, was the outer parlour – the only place where monks could meet visitors. However, over time, this range was gradually taken over and rebuilt by successive abbots to provide suitably grand accommodation for themselves, their household staff and distinguished guests. Mitred abbots of Battle, members of the House of Lords, were powerful men and major landholders in the region. As such they would have entertained distinguished visitors and their officials. The west range was rebuilt in the thirteenth century in order to meet these needs, and included a first-floor hall and other accommodation specifically designed for entertaining. The range was later extended to

accommodate a larger ground-floor hall, reflecting the arrangements in the grander secular residences of the time. At the Dissolution of the Monasteries in the sixteenth century, little needed to be done to convert it to a private house and it remained as such until the 1920s.

The highest roof with the stepped gables and cross is the later great hall, built in the fifteenth century. In front of it is the main entrance to the west range with the abbot's great chamber above. To the right is the library wing designed by Henry Clutton and built in the late 1850s. The space between the library and the twin octagonal towers to the west (beyond the tennis courts) is the site of the guest range. This was extensively modernised by Sir Anthony Browne in the late 1530s; the towers are all that remain of his work but below, accessible from the lower terrace, are medieval vaults.

*Carry on down the path past the gatehouse.*

*On the right, just behind the trees, is an exhibition and a short video explaining the events leading to up the Battle of Hastings.*

*Follow the path round to a terrace; a sign on the right marks the start of the battlefield walk.*

*This path crosses the battlefield, rejoining the abbey tour near the monks' latrine block. Along the route, information panels describe the course of the battle, while from the far side there are spectacular view of Battle Abbey. The bird's eye view on the inside front cover shows the route to take.*

*Visitors just wishing to see the abbey should continue along the terrace and rejoin the main route at the far end.*

*The interior of the abbot's great hall in 1783. This is open to visitors only during the school's summer holidays*

*Annotated engraving of the west range of the abbey cloister looking across the site of the monastic kitchen and the refectory from the south-east*

*The interior of the abbot's great hall today. The roof and timbers of this fifteenth-century hall were replaced after the fire of 1931*

THE SOUTH-WEST VIEW OF BATTEL-ABBEY, IN THE COUNTY OF SUSSEX.

*This engraving of Battle Abbey by the Buck Brothers, of 1737, provides a fine view of the now largely vanished guest range and part of the precinct wall*

*The heavily buttressed vaulted undercrofts of the monastic guest house. The octagonal tower forms part of Sir Anthony Browne's rebuilding works of the early 1540s. (The steps are nineteenth-century)*

## THE TERRACE, THE BARN AND THE GUEST RANGE

The terrace walk, overlooking the heart of the battlefield, was laid out in its present form for Lady Webster, probably in the 1820s. The blocked window and large doorway in the wall on the left belong to a monastic barn, which was once on the south-west extremity of the outer court.

*Carry on along the terrace until you reach a doorway on the left.*

This door leads to a series of thirteenth-century vaulted undercrofts belonging to the monastic guest range. These would mostly have been store rooms.

*Go through the door.*

Inside, on the right, there is a medieval corner fireplace with a damaged hood – an indication that this room was used as an office or workshop.

*When you have finished exploring the undercrofts, go back out of the door and turn left, carrying along the terrace. Stop when you reach the remains of the dormitory and the latrine block. Those who have come from the battlefield walk, carry straight on up the path and stop by the information panel opposite the dormitory.*

## THE EAST RANGE

The east range of the cloister contained the monks' dormitory on the first floor with a series of rooms below. Dramatic evidence of the difficulties of building on this narrow ridge is provided by the heavily buttressed southern half of the building which towers over the surrounding ground. Its height was necessary to allow the first-floor dormitory to be at one level and to give reasonable head-room in the ground-floor rooms at the northern end.

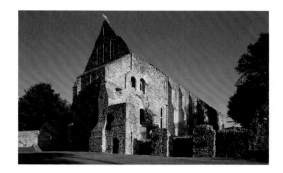

## THE LATRINE BLOCK

To the right of the dormitory are the remains of the latrine block, known as the 'reredorter'. This once stood to the same height as the dormitory, allowing the monks direct access from their sleeping quarters. The line of stone arches which forms the south wall once supported a row of latrine seats at first-floor level. Directly below was the main drain.

A good water supply was of great importance to a monastery, where hygiene tended to be well in advance of the outside world. Wherever possible, an ample supply of clean water was channelled through the monastery, providing relatively pure supplies for the kitchen, abbot's residence, *lavatorium* (cloister basins) and infirmary, before flushing the latrines. Battle Abbey's hilltop site made a running-water supply a particular problem. While there was enough for most domestic purposes there must be doubts that there was an adequate supply for effectively cleansing the latrines. It is possible that the latrine block periodically had to be cleared out like a medieval cesspit. The arches carrying the first-floor latrine seats might have been constructed in this way in order to save the cost of a solid wall, but the absence of a contained channel below suggests that they could equally well have been built to allow access for cleaning the drain.

*Turn back towards the terrace and go up the steps on the right. Go through the first door on the right into the novices' chamber.*

## THE NOVICES' CHAMBER

This lofty, vaulted room at the southern end of the east range is one of the finest medieval chambers in the abbey, its height not so much a reflection of its own importance but necessary to give a level first floor to the dormitory above, which runs the full length of the building. A single row of marble columns carries the vaults and divides the room into two bays in width. In the south-east corner a narrow stairway leads to a latrine. The wide windows on either side of the entrance probably held plate tracery; that to the north has subsequently been altered. In the south wall are the remains of a substantial fireplace, the marks of its hood clearly visible above the tiled fireback. Smoke from the fire went into a hollow buttress outside. (The presence of this fireplace indicates that this must have been a room of some importance.) The position of the room suggests that it might have been used by the young novice, or trainee, monks.

*Climb the wooden stairs in the corner of the room, into a small vaulted room. Go through the next doorway.*

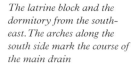

*The latrine block and the dormitory from the south-east. The arches along the south side mark the course of the main drain*

*The novices' chamber in the east range of the cloister. The height of the vaulting indicates the problems of building on a steeply sloping site*

*A reconstruction drawing of the novices' chamber in the east range as it might have appeared in the twelfth century, by Peter Urmston*

*Left: A view of the interior of the monks' common room*

*Right: The east range of the cloister from the north-east. The upper floor was the monks' dormitory. In the foreground is the curved end of the eleventh-century chapter house*

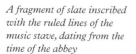

*A fragment of slate inscribed with the ruled lines of the music stave, dating from the time of the abbey*

## THE SLYPE

This barrel-vaulted passage was the main route from the cloister to the infirmary buildings to the east. (The outline of what may be part of the infirmary lies to the north of the later ice house and dairy.) A doorway in the north wall leads to the monks' common room.

## THE COMMON ROOM

This is one of the most ornate of the abbey's rooms, still containing its medieval carved corbels (projecting stones used to support the springing of the vaulted ceiling) in the shape of animal and human heads on the walls. Its location suggests that it was used as the monks' common room. It would probably have been heated in the winter by portable charcoal braziers. The room is lit by five pointed, arched windows (known as lancet windows) while the main doorway gives direct access to the cloister on the opposite side.

*Go up the stairs, out of the common room, and turn right.*

Right next to this room are the roofless remains of the inner parlour.

## THE INNER PARLOUR

This was one of the very few places where monks were allowed to talk, silence being the general rule. It was once a rectangular room with a vaulted ceiling and stone benches along the main walls (traces of these remain). A doorway at its eastern end led to the infirmary. The two doors into the common room are twentieth-century.

*Carry on along the path to the chapter house.*

## THE CHAPTER HOUSE

Along with the church, the chapter house was the centre of formal abbey life. Here the abbot and monks met each day to discuss the business of their community and to listen to a reading from a chapter of the Benedictine Rule. It was originally a simple building with a semicircular end, completed around 1100. Within, a number of graves were found in the floor. It was later remodelled during the life of the monastery and new windows were inserted. The original shallow benching round the walls still survives.

*Turn round and look back up at the dormitory.*

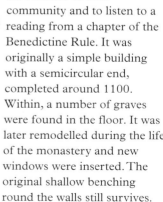

BRITISH LIBRARY

## THE DORMITORY

All the first floor of the eastern range was the monks' dormitory, known as the 'dorter'. Its scale is best appreciated from near the chapter house. Lit by a series of lancet windows with shutters at the bottom, its interior was second only to the church in size. Originally, this great austere room would have been open from end to end, its white plastered walls relieved by red-painted masonry joints. However, there is evidence, most notably in the form of inserted fireplaces and a small window at the south end of the west wall, to suggest that it was partitioned at a later date, a common development in monastic houses. Such partitions, lightly constructed and leaving no trace, would have formed a series of individual cubicles opening from a wide central corridor.

Access to the dormitory was via an external staircase at the northern end of the west wall; only the doorway remains together with a scar in the wall marking the position of the stairs. The sloping ground makes it unlikely that there was a passage over the chapter house to the night-stairs in the church, so this staircase leading from the cloister to the dormitory almost certainly had to be used by the monks on their way to night-time services. The small spiral staircase projecting from the east wall probably gave access to the roof. In 1369 the roof was covered in wooden shingles but by the time of the Dissolution in the sixteenth century these had been replaced with tiles. The building remained roofed until the end of the eighteenth century; it was then converted into stables, approached by an earth ramp at the north end.

## THE SOUTH RANGE

The site of the south range is not open to visitors but it is best seen from outside the chapter house. It was entirely occupied by the dining hall, known as the 'frater', the outline of which is marked out in the grass. The stub of its south wall can be seen projecting from the west range with evidence of a first-floor window. Along its former west wall are the remains of decorative stonework – probably indicative of the high end of the hall where the abbot would have sat. South of the dining hall and also marked out in the grass is the outline of the great kitchen which was demolished between 1683 and 1687.

## THE CLOISTER WALK

The cloister walk, marked by gravel paths, linked the buildings of the cloister and provided the monks with a sheltered area for exercise. Initially, it was probably protected by a simple pentice or lean-to roof, but under Abbot Walter de Luci (1139–71) it was rebuilt with pavements and columns of marble. Throughout the Middle Ages it was further modified and rebuilt.

*Carry on up the path and go through the screen of trees to the abbey church.*

*Above left: A nineteenth-century view of the east range from the south-west. In the foreground is part of the elaborate gardens that were developed by the Duke and Duchess of Cleveland*

*Above: A reconstruction drawing showing the north walk of the cloister as it might have appeared in the late thirteenth century, by Peter Urmston. The sunny northern walks were often used for activities such as writing*

*Left: The south end of the dormitory range. This was extensively reconstructed in the thirteenth century. To the right are the arches of the latrine*

*Medieval prickers used by the monks for book production. These instruments were used to make fine pin-holes in the parchment to enable accurate lines to be ruled*

## THE ABBEY CHURCH

The abbey church was completely destroyed immediately after the Dissolution in 1538, and little remains to be seen, although the original east end, with the presumed site of the high altar marking the spot where King Harold was killed, has been indicated on the ground. In the early nineteenth century, the crypt chapels were excavated, and limited investigation in the 1930s and more recently has enabled a plan of the church to be deduced with some accuracy. However, an effort of imagination is needed to visualise what was once the focus and heart of the community.

The original church was probably begun in 1070/1 and completed in 1094. It was an aisled building, with a nave of seven bays, and it was some 65 metres (225 feet) long, equalling the great contemporary churches of Normandy in size. Although modest in scale compared to the second generation of post-Conquest churches in England, it was probably the first in this country to combine a semicircular ambulatory (an aisle around the east end of the church), with chapels radiating out from it.

However, late in the thirteenth century when the remodelling of the cloister buildings was almost complete, the monks turned their attention to the church. By then, what had undoubtedly seemed magnificent and modern in the 1090s probably appeared cramped and old-fashioned. To meet changing requirements and tastes, the church east of the crossing and transepts was demolished and replaced by a new seven-bay choir 46 metres (152 feet) long. It had a polygonal east end with five radiating chapels, a design probably derived from Henry III's rebuilding of Westminster Abbey between 1246 and 1259. The sloping site allowed for a vaulted eastern crypt; three chapels forming part of this were excavated in 1817 and can be seen.

*Walk past the site of the high altar and look down the slope to see the remains of the crypt.*

In the north and south chapels are 'piscinas' – carved basins in the walls for washing sacred vessels.

## THE DAIRY AND ICE HOUSE

South-east of the church lie a thatched dairy and ice house, built by Sir Godfrey Vassall Webster soon after he inherited the estate in 1810. Dairies such as this, separate from the kitchens of country houses, became very fashionable in the eighteenth century and examples can be traced back to the 1730s. Many owners built them in a Classical or, as here, in a Gothick style.

The walls of the dairy are double-skinned to keep the interior cool. The coloured glass windows, together with the perforated zinc screens to keep out birds and insects, are based on surviving fragments found on site (the building was restored in 1991). Inside, the stone benches have nearly all been replaced, but the floor tiles are mostly original. To the south (at the back of the building) lies the ruined scullery used for cleaning and scalding the equipment.

The low mound next to the dairy conceals an ice house, which may be contemporary with the dairy. A short passage leads to the ice house, with double sets of doors forming air-locks to help maintain the low temperature. As was usual, it lies almost entirely below ground level to help insulation, and is built of brick and shaped like an egg. A drain at the bottom allowed the melt-water to disperse. Ice houses were introduced into England during the latter part of the seventeenth century; they only went out of use when they were superseded by mechanical refrigeration late in the nineteenth century. In the winter, estate workers would have packed the ice house with blocks of ice from the ponds in the valley. This ice could last all through the following summer, providing a supply both for the house and to help cool the adjacent dairy.

*Walk back towards the site of the high altar and carry straight on until you reach the precinct wall.*

## THE PRECINCT WALL

The medieval precinct wall once enclosed the whole monastery. It is unusual in having a wall-walk for defensive purposes, which in its present form is probably contemporary with the fourteenth-century gatehouse. From the wall-walk there is a good view of the town and the parish church.

*Follow the path round until you come back to the gatehouse where the tour began.*

*Above: Entrance to the nineteenth-century ice house*

*Below: Part of the medieval precinct wall. Battle Abbey is unusual for a monastery in having a wall-walk. This defensive feature may reflect the threat of French raids in the fourteenth century*

# THE BATTLE OF HASTINGS, 1066

~ THE BATTLE OF HASTINGS IS UNDOUBTEDLY THE MOST CELEBRATED BATTLE TO HAVE BEEN FOUGHT ON ENGLISH SOIL.

BRITISH LIBRARY, BL53004

*William the Conqueror, depicted as a medieval knight riding with his soldiers, from an early fourteenth-century manuscript*

*Silver penny minted during Ethelred's reign*

*Silver penny minted during Cnut's reign*

## THE SIGNIFICANCE OF THE BATTLE

On Saturday 14 October 1066, the armies of Harold of England and William of Normandy fought for the throne of England. William's victory marked a turning-point in English history, as the Normans imposed a new political order on the country. This was to have a profound and lasting impact on the development of English society, culture, religion and government.

## THE SOURCES

Trying to reconstruct what actually happened in 1066 involves some careful detective work. We are completely reliant on the *Bayeux Tapestry* and various written descriptions of the Norman Conquest for our knowledge of the battle. Confusingly, these accounts offer contradictory information about some vital events. Moreover, the most important sources are pro-Norman, eulogising William and his actions, and in one case comparing him with great heroes of Antiquity. Trying to reconcile these conflicting accounts is extremely problematic. As a result, the history of the battle and the events leading up to it have become the source

BRITISH MUSEUM

of endless discussion and disagreement amongst scholars. Particularly controversial is the issue of why William won: was his army more professional than that of Harold, or was he a better leader? Or did luck play a part on that fateful day in 1066?

## ENGLAND BEFORE THE CONQUEST

In 976, King Ethelred acceded to the English throne. His long reign was so characterized by disaster and instability that he was given the nickname 'Unraed', meaning 'uncounselled', in punning reference to his name, which means 'the wise counsellor'. Taking advantage of this instability, the Vikings began raiding England and extracting huge ransoms called Danegeld in return for the promise of a peaceful withdrawal. In 1002, Ethelred married Emma, the sister of Robert, duke of Normandy. The Vikings had used the Normandy coast as a base for their operations and it is possible that by making this match Ethelred hoped to end this practice.

Despite this Norman alliance, Ethelred's kingdom continued to crumble under the pressure of repeated Viking attacks and when Ethelred died in

BRITISH MUSEUM

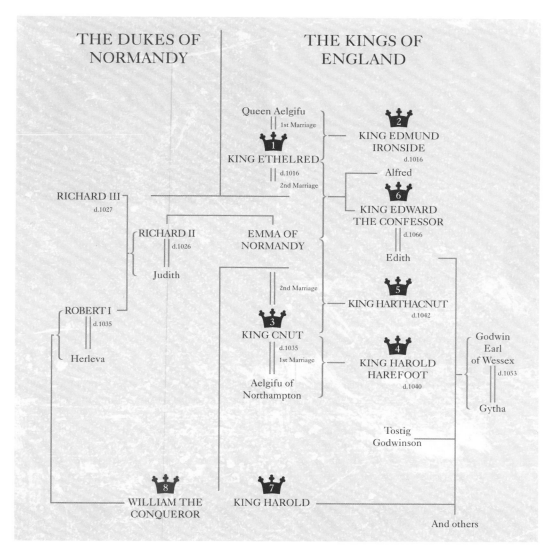

## THE DUKES OF NORMANDY

## THE KINGS OF ENGLAND

Queen Aelgifu
┃┃ 1st Marriage

**👑 2**
**KING EDMUND IRONSIDE**
d.1016

**👑 1**
**KING ETHELRED**
┃┃ d.1016
2nd Marriage

Alfred

**👑 6**
**KING EDWARD THE CONFESSOR**
┃┃ d.1066

RICHARD III
d.1027

RICHARD II
┃┃ d.1026

EMMA OF NORMANDY

Edith

Judith

2nd Marriage

**👑 5**
**KING HARTHACNUT**
d.1042

ROBERT I
┃┃ d.1035

**👑 3**
**KING CNUT**
d.1035
1st Marriage

**👑 4**
**KING HAROLD HAREFOOT**
d.1040

Godwin Earl of Wessex
d.1053

Herleva

Aelgifu of Northampton

Gytha

Tostig Godwinson

**👑 8**
**WILLIAM THE CONQUEROR**

**👑 7**
**KING HAROLD**

And others

*This family tree demonstrates William's blood relationship with Edward the Confessor, and his claim on the English throne*

*Edward the Confessor and Harthacnut with their mother, Emma of Normandy, from a mid-eleventh-century account of Emma's life. The scribe is shown kneeling in the foreground, presenting the manuscript to Emma*

1016, Cnut, the brother of the king of Denmark, seized the English throne. Ethelred's heir, Edmund Ironside, a son by his first marriage, died later that year resisting Cnut, and his two remaining sons by Emma of Normandy, Alfred and Edward, fled from the new king to their mother's homeland. To prevent the duke of Normandy supporting their claims to the English crown, Cnut then married Emma himself.

At his death in 1035, Cnut had one legitimate son by Emma, Harthacnut, and one illegitimate son by a mistress, Harold Harefoot. Harthacnut was the heir to the kingdoms of both Denmark and England, but the threat of an invasion of Denmark by the Norwegian king prevented him from claiming the English crown immediately. This created a power vacuum in England and, in his absence, his three step-brothers, Harold Harefoot, Alfred and Edward, manœuvred for the crown. Harold Harefoot was the victor: he murdered Alfred and drove Edward back into exile.

In 1040 Harold Harefoot died and Harthacnut, who had been preparing to invade England, came to the throne peaceably. He in turn died in 1042 without an heir, and Emma of Normandy's last surviving son, Edward (known as the Confessor), returned from his Norman exile to be crowned king.

Quite how Edward came to the throne was disputed by contemporaries. Norman

*13*

HISTORISK MUSEET STOCKHOLME.T.ARCHIVE

*Above: A ninth-century Viking picture stone from Gotland, showing warriors fighting and a ship*

*Above right: Edward the Confessor dining in state, from a fourteenth-century manuscript*

BRITISH LIBRARY/COT.A.XIII.F.3

sources claim that William the Conqueror was instrumental in ensuring his accession, but English accounts credit it to the industry of Earl Godwin, a nobleman who had raised himself to great power and prominence in the reigns of Harold Harefoot and Harthacnut. Whatever the case, Earl Godwin and his sons, Harold and Tostig, came to dominate Edward the Confessor's court and in 1045 the king married Edith, the daughter of the earl.

Edward's marriage to Edith was childless and as he grew older the question of who would inherit the throne became increasingly urgent. It is recorded by Norman authors that William the Conqueror had been promised the English throne by Edward the Confessor and that to quiet fears of a disputed succession Harold, the son of Earl Godwin, was sent to Normandy to confirm this pledge on the king's behalf. Harold's journey is depicted in great detail on the *Bayeux Tapestry* – a pro-Norman record of events – where he is shown taking a solemn oath to William over some relics. The terms of this oath are recorded by William of Poitiers, William the Conqueror's chaplain. According to him, Harold willingly swore to help William accede to the throne and acknowledged him as his feudal lord.

Although scholars are generally agreed that Harold did visit Normandy, probably in 1064, it is curious that no contemporary Anglo-Saxon source mentions either this journey or the oath. Both are mentioned, however, in later accounts, sympathetic to Harold's cause, but these insist that the oath was taken under duress. Since William was later to emphasise Edward's promise and Harold's oath as the principal justifications for his succession to the throne, the facts of this matter are of vital importance, but we have no means of ascertaining the truth of what actually happened.

In 1065, shortly after these events are believed to have taken place, there was a rebellion in the north of England against Harold's brother, Tostig, who had been installed

*A scene from the* Bayeux Tapestry *showing Harold swearing an oath to William*

© MICHAEL HOLFORD

as earl of Northumbria.

Harold was sent to mediate with the rebels but their strength convinced him that attempting to restore his brother would cause civil war. As a result, King Edward was forced to banish Tostig. According to the *Vita Edwardi*, some people accused Harold of instigating the rebellion in order to get rid of his brother.

On 5 January 1066 King Edward died childless. Whatever his earlier intentions, it is probable that, on his deathbed, he nominated Harold as his successor. Harold acted swiftly and, with the support of the Witan, the grand council of England, had himself crowned the very next day. There was good reason for this speed. He must have realised that the throne would be contested by three formidable powers: the Danish descendants of King Cnut; Harold's disgruntled brother in exile, Tostig; and William, who said he had been promised the throne and could lay claim to the succession through Emma of Normandy.

*Above left: William I, as depicted in the twelfth-century* Battle Chronicle

*Above: Portraits of the first four Norman kings of England, each holding a model of a church he founded, from* Historia Anglorum *by Matthew Parris (d.1259)*

THE BATTLE OF HASTINGS

*Harold's coronation, from the* Bayeux Tapestry

*Right: Falaise Castle in Normandy, the birthplace of William the Conqueror*

## WILLIAM OF NORMANDY

William's career before 1066 was remarkable. The illegitimate son of Duke Robert of Normandy, he succeeded to the duchy in 1035 when he was only seven or eight years old. The anarchy in Normandy in his early years helped to make him into a determined and ruthless soldier. It is said that, when he was besieging Alençon in 1051, the citizens of the town taunted him for being the illegitimate son of an undertaker's daughter. When the town fell, he took his revenge by having the hands and feet of some of the citizens cut off. His military prowess and his qualities as a leader were constantly tested and it was not until 1060 that he was in secure control of his duchy. By the time he was ready to assert his claim to the throne of England, he was a seasoned soldier with a highly successful record, who had not only gained complete mastery of his Norman inheritance but had also added to his dominions.

## THE YEAR 1066

The *Anglo-Saxon Chronicle* records that, at Easter, 'over all England there was seen a sign in the skies such as had never been seen before'. The arrival of Halley's Comet suggested to contemporaries that great things were about to happen. William of Poitiers, writing after the event, describes it as an omen of the invasion. Harold was certainly aware of the potential danger from Normandy, and in April or May he moved down to the Isle of Wight where, according to the *Anglo-Saxon Chronicle*, 'he assembled a naval force and a land force larger than any king had assembled before in this country'.

However, he was also conscious of the threat from his

brother Tostig. It was Tostig who posed the first challenge to Harold's rule. While exiled in Flanders, Tostig had gathered a fleet of some sixty ships with which he raided the coast of England, gradually working his way round to the mouth of the Humber. On one of his raids, his force was defeated by Earl Edwin of Mercia, and he was forced to flee to Scotland with only twelve ships.

William, meanwhile, had been trying to prepare to invade England. At first, he found it difficult to gain the support of the powerful lords of Normandy because they regarded his enterprise as foolhardy. However, many owed him their positions of power and were tempted

*Below right: The appearance of Halley's Comet, from the Bayeux Tapestry*

*Below: Equestrian statue of William the Conqueror at Falaise in Normandy*

by the rich rewards that a successful conquest of England would bring. The existing Norman fleet was not large enough to carry the required men and horses across the Channel, so William required each of his supporters to provide him with a specified number of ships. A near-contemporary text records that William's half-brothers, Robert, count of Mortain, and Bishop Odo of Bayeux, were responsible for providing 120 and 100 ships respectively and a number of other lords were required to provide at least sixty each. William's magnates also brought their own troops recruited from all over France. From May onwards the invasion fleet was being assembled in the Dives estuary in Normandy and by early August it was ready. William also received support from the Pope, who gave him a banner which was carried in the van of the Norman army.

The wind was unfavourable, however, so the fleet was forced to wait until it changed. Some six weeks later, William set sail from the Dives estuary to St Valéry-sur-Somme along the coast, but, in doing so, he lost some of his ships which were blown onto the lee shore by the westerly wind. William's action has been interpreted by some as a calculated move to shorten his eventual Channel crossing. But it is also possible that, in order to quell impatience and unrest among his troops, William attempted to launch his invasion at this time and only avoided disaster in increasingly bad weather by running for cover in the Somme estuary.

Harold was also in difficulty at this time. The *Anglo-Saxon Chronicle* reveals that on 8 September he was forced to disband his army and order his fleet back to London because their provisions were exhausted. This left the south coast undefended. Early in September, the king of Norway, Harold Hardraada, arrived off the Tyne with an invasion fleet of approximately 300 ships. There he was joined by Tostig with the small contingent of ships that he was able to bring from Scotland. The combined force sailed up the Humber and landed at Riccall not far from York. On 20 September, in a bloody battle at Fulford, Hardraada and Tostig defeated an

army led by King Harold's supporters, Earl Edwin of Mercia and his brother Earl Morcar of Northumbria. The invaders then took York.

Harold resolved to confront Hardraada and Tostig. He rapidly assembled an army and marched north with astonishing speed, covering 190 miles in just five days. On 25 September he caught the greater part of Tostig's army completely by surprise at Stamford Bridge, and he won a resounding victory. Both Hardraada and Tostig were killed and the invaders needed only twenty-four of their 300 ships to carry the survivors back to Norway. Harold had recovered control of the north of England but he had little time to savour his victory. A few days later he received the news that William of Normandy had landed.

## WILLIAM'S INVASION

On 27 September the wind in the Channel at last began to blow from the south. William hastily embarked his troops and set sail at nightfall. His own ship carried a lantern at its masthead but, despite this, he lost touch with the rest of his fleet during the night crossing, and in the morning his ship stood alone in an empty sea. William calmed the nerves of his crew by having a leisurely meal as though nothing was wrong. As he finished his meal, the rest of the fleet came in sight and later that day his forces landed unopposed at Pevensey.

William ordered the old Roman fort at Pevensey to be fortified, and on 29 September he moved the bulk of his forces along the coast to Hastings. This move suggests that he had probably landed further to the west than he had

# THE BATTLE OF HASTINGS

*Above left: The Norman fleet crosses the Channel, from the Bayeux Tapestry*

*The Normans drag their ships out to sea, from the Bayeux Tapestry*

intended. Once at Hastings, William again constructed a castle and then began pillaging the local countryside in order to feed his troops. Surprisingly, he remained in the Hastings area for the next fortnight rather than taking advantage of Harold's absence in the north to march on London or seize one of the southern towns such as Dover, Canterbury or Winchester. Historians have speculated as to why he did not move, and various explanations about his tactics have been put forward. It may be that he wanted to stay close to his fleet, in case he had to make a swift escape. Alternatively, the pillaging of the local

countryside – much of it Harold's ancestral land – could have been a calculated and deliberate provocation, designed to force Harold to make the first move.

News of William's landing reached Harold at the end of September while he was still in York. He travelled south rapidly, summoning new troops as he went. He reached London at the end of the first week in October and rested for a few days while he gathered reinforcements. On about 11 October he moved south to confront William in Sussex. His rapid movements have been variously interpreted as an attempt to take the Normans by surprise; as an angry response to William's pillaging of his ancestral property; or simply over-confidence. Whatever the case, it meant that his forces were not properly assembled before Hastings; in particular he lacked bowmen, possibly because they did not have time to march south from Stamford Bridge. Meanwhile, he also mobilised his fleet, in order to cut off William's retreat by sea.

Harold's army reached its rendezvous, a local Sussex landmark described in the *Anglo-Saxon Chronicle* as 'the hoary apple-tree', in the evening of 13 October. This was probably Caldbec Hill, near the modern town of Battle and about a mile from the battlefield. It is possible that, at this stage, Harold intended to wait until his full forces arrived. He probably thought that he had a large enough army to contain a Norman attack in Hastings and he could destroy the invaders at leisure in a combined land and sea assault once he was strong enough. If so, he must have been taken by surprise by his enemy's bold stroke the following morning. William, having kept his army on alert all night in case of a sudden English attack, at once seized the initiative. At dawn on 14 October he marched his troops the seven miles north from Hastings to confront Harold. According to the *Anglo-Saxon Chronicle*, 'William came against him by surprise before his army was drawn up in battle array.' Once Harold heard that the Normans were on the move, he quickly arranged his army in a strong defensive position along Senlac Ridge.

*A map of England and Normandy in 1066*

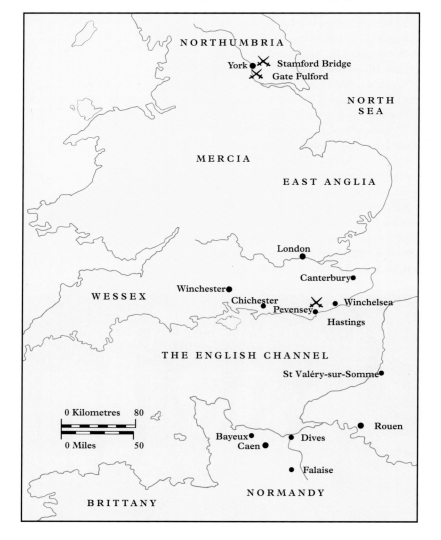

## THE OPENING PHASE OF THE BATTLE

William's army was probably positioned on the lower slope, opposite the ridge where Harold's forces gathered. The Normans occupied the centre, the Bretons took up their positions on the left with the Flemings probably on the right. In the front rank were the archers, behind them were the infantry and in the third rank were the cavalry. Harold's army formed a dense shield wall that might have been anything from three or four to ten or twelve men deep and stretching for about 800 yards along the ridge. Harold's housecarls grouped themselves around his standard and formed the centre of the line. It is possible that Harold placed his brothers Gyrth and Leofwine, with their housecarls, on each of the flanks. The well-armoured housecarls would probably have been in the first few ranks with the fyrd men behind them.

The battle is reckoned to have begun at about 9 am when William ordered his archers forward, to fire at the English line. He then sent in his infantry, and some time later, the cavalry to support them. There was fierce fighting, but the attack foundered. The English exploited their excellent defensive position and their axemen and javelin throwers inflicted heavy losses.

*Above: The battle formation, seen from behind the Norman lines, looking towards Harold's army who were positioned on the ridge. Reconstruction drawing by Peter Dunn*

*Below: The first Norman attack on the English shield wall. Reconstruction drawing by Peter Dunn*

19

# THE OPPOSING FORCES

There has been endless speculation as to the numbers involved in the conflict. We cannot be sure of the actual figures, but it is likely that there were approximately 7,000 men on each side. William's army probably comprised about 4,000 Normans, supplemented by about 1,500 Flemings and 2,000 Bretons. Of this total, roughly 2,000 would have been cavalry, 4,000 infantry and 1,500 archers.

The backbone of Harold's army was his contingent of about 1,000 housecarls, his own and those of his brothers, Gyrth and Leofwine. Housecarls were professional warriors who were attached to the king's household. They were household retainers who performed administrative and law-enforcement tasks in peacetime, as well as fighting for their lord in war. The bulk of the English army was drawn from the 'fyrd'. This was a levy of men from the kingdom at large. Each community, landed estate, town and even religious house was required to provide one man for every five hides of land it possessed. (A hide was between 60 and 120 acres.)

*Artist's impression of a Saxon thane, by Peter Dunn*

*Artist's impression of a Norman knight, by Peter Dunn*

# THE SOLDIERS' ARMOUR

As the *Bayeux Tapestry* shows, the principal soldiers on each side had similar armour. They wore conical helmets with a nose-piece at the front and heavy mail shirts, called hauberks, which covered the torso and thighs. In the scene in the tapestry in which William's equipment is being loaded onto his ships, each hauberk has to be carried aboard by two men, as they were so heavy. Hauberks were clearly valuable, and there are scenes in the tapestry of fallen men being stripped of them by soldiers without armour. Most of the soldiers shown in the tapestry are carrying kite-shaped shields, rounded at the top, pointed at the bottom and large enough to protect the body and the legs. Some of the English soldiers are shown carrying smaller, round shields. William's archers (with one exception) and some of Harold's soldiers, possibly the fyrdmen, are shown dressed in tunics not armour, reflecting their lower social status. However, unarmoured English soldiers appear in only two scenes of the tapestry, and one of those depicts the English fleeing at the end of the battle. So it is quite possible that even some of Harold's fyrd, the body of the army, were well equipped, in which case they would be indistinguishable from the housecarls in the tapestry. There is little doubt that Harold and his housecarls travelled to battle on horseback (he and his men could scarcely have made their epic journeys to and from York otherwise) but they always fought on foot, in the Viking tradition.

The Norman knights were armed with swords and spears. Their swords were designed for slashing rather than piercing, and they had two different types of spears. One type was used for throwing, like a javelin, the other for thrusting. Although William's archers were to play a crucial role in the battle, it is clear from the tapestry that shields provided considerable protection from their arrows. Harold's army at Hastings lacked archers (the tapestry gives him just one) but his principal soldiers used similar weapons to the Normans. Their distinctive asset was the axe, a massive weapon that had to be wielded with two hands.

1. *Norman sword*
2. *English sword*
3. *Norman lance*
4. *English spear*
5. *Norman spur*
6. *Two-handed English axe*

*Above left: The Normans carrying their hauberks aboard the fleet, from the Bayeux Tapestry*

*Left: Norman archers, from the Bayeux Tapestry*

## THE CRISIS OF THE BATTLE

After perhaps an hour's fighting, William's Breton cavalry, on the left of the Norman line, began to break and retreat and this started a panic among his entire force. The extent of the crisis is acknowledged even by William's foremost apologist, the Norman chronicler, William of Poitiers:

*Frightened by such [English] ferocity, the infantry and Breton mounted warriors both retreated, with all the auxiliary troops who formed the left wing. Almost the whole of the Duke's army yielded. The Normans believed that their duke and lord had been killed. Their retreat was not a shameful flight but a sorrowful withdrawal.*

For some commentators, this crisis provided Harold with an opportunity to win the day. Had he ordered his entire army to advance he might have turned the Norman retreat into a rout. It could be argued that his lack of cavalry was decisive at this moment, although it is also possible that a disciplined infantry advance alone might have defeated William's demoralised and disordered knights. The *Bayeux Tapestry* suggests that it was around this time that

Harold's brothers, Gyrth and Leofwine, were killed.

The crisis certainly brought out the best in William. His response is described by William of Poitiers:

*The prince, seeing the greater part of the enemy camp setting out in pursuit of his men, hurled himself in front of the fugitives, and stopped them by striking them or menacing them with his spear. Then, having uncovered his head and taken off his helmet, he shouted: "Look at me! I am alive, and will be the victor, with God's help! What madness induces you to flee? What avenue of retreat is open to you? Those whom you could have slaughtered like sheep have driven you back and are killing you! You are deserting victory and inextinguishable glory to lose yourselves in flight and eternal shame! By fleeing none of you will escape death." With these words they regained courage.*

By rallying his men, William was able to counterattack. Those English soldiers who had broken ranks and charged down from the hill after the retreating Normans were now encircled and killed.

## THE BATTLE OF HASTINGS

*Below: William lifts his helmet to show that he is still alive, from the* Bayeux Tapestry

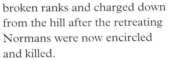

*After ferocious fighting, the Norman attack hesitates and breaks. Reconstruction drawing by Peter Dunn*

# THE NORMANS' STAGED RETREATS

By regrouping his army William had prevented defeat, but he was still no nearer to winning. Harold had perhaps lost an opportunity to win and his shield wall was undoubtedly weaker, but he still commanded a strong army that retained its seemingly impregnable defensive position. William launched more attacks up the hill to try to dislodge the English. It was during this stage of the battle that the Normans are said to have carried out a series of manœuvres which seem to have won them the battle. In the middle of an attack, they would suddenly pretend to retreat, prompting the English to break ranks in pursuit. The Normans would then suddenly wheel round and counterattack the English. Interestingly, this tactic is described in accounts of other battles fought by the Normans, but it is not clear how it was done at Hastings. It seems unlikely that William's entire cavalry carried out the manœuvre together, rather that small detachments did so, each time drawing off a small section of Harold's army. In this way, Harold's army was gradually weakened, although it still held its line along the ridge.

*Modern stained-glass window commemorating the Battle of Hastings in St Mary's Church, Battle*

BRITISH LIBRARY/COTT. VITT. A.XIII.F. 3V

*A fourteenth-century manuscript illustration showing William killing Harold in a duel – a later interpretation of the Battle of Hastings*

*The Normans pretend to flee, and then they suddenly wheel round and pursue the English who have broken ranks to chase them. Reconstruction drawing by Peter Dunn*

## THE FINAL ASSAULT

In the evening, possibly as late as 7 pm, William regrouped his forces for what proved to be the final assault on the English position. Again he sent his archers forward first. One later source says that William ordered them to shoot their arrows high into the air so that they came down on the heads of the English. However, this claim is not supported by the contemporary sources nor is it evident from the tapestry. Perhaps William's archers were simply more successful than they had been in the morning because the intensity of the fighting had gradually weakened the shield wall. His troops

pursued by Norman knights. Significantly, the retreating English are depicted without armour.

By the time night fell, the Norman victory was complete. It is possible that at this time some Norman knights, chasing the English through the gathering gloom, rode into a deep ditch – known as the Malfosse – and suffered heavy losses as the fleeing English turned on them. The contemporary sources are ambiguous about the incident and modern

*William's archers, some of whom might have used crossbows, fire at the English line in preparation for the final attack. Reconstruction drawing by Peter Dunn*

*The scene from the* Bayeux Tapestry, *showing Harold being hit in the eye by an arrow and then being cut down by a Norman knight*

then broke the English line and a great slaughter began as the evening drew in.

It was at around this time that Harold was killed. The *Bayeux Tapestry* is the only contemporary source which describes the manner of his death. This much-debated scene is generally agreed to show Harold being hit in the eye by an arrow and then being cut down. Harold's death must have demoralised the English. The final scene of the tapestry shows the English fleeing and being vigorously

William's army finally
breaks through the English
line at dusk. Reconstruction
drawing by Peter Dunn

The English flee, pursued by
the Normans, from the
Bayeux Tapestry

ET FVGA VE R TERVNT

The Body of Harold Brought Before William *(1844–61) by Ford Madox Brown. William is said to have refused to allow him a proper burial.*

historians are divided about when and where it occurred. It is even possible that the incident happened during, rather than after, the battle, and that this is what is depicted in the scene in the tapestry in which a group of English soldiers on a hillock are enjoying some success against the Norman knights.

Probably the next day, the grisly business of burying the dead began. Harold's brothers were found but the king himself could not be identified because his face had been so mutilated. Legend has it that his mistress, Edith Swan-Neck, identified him by recognising distinctive marks on his body. William is said to have refused the request of Harold's mother to remove his body and bury it, even though she offered his weight in gold. He believed that, as an oath-breaker, Harold had lost his claim to an honourable burial and he ordered that the body be buried on the sea-shore. It is likely that his remains were moved soon afterwards to Waltham Abbey in Essex.

*Silver penny minted during William's reign*

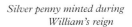

*View of Battle Abbey from the battlefield. This was later to be part of the abbey's Great Park*

## AN INEVITABLE RESULT?

Although the two armies were similar in terms of size and equipment, the important difference between them was that the Normans possessed cavalry and archers whereas the English did not. Some historians have concluded from this that the English army was out of date and that its defeat by the Normans, led by a superior general and using more modern military techniques, was inevitable, but this view cannot be sustained. Harold's generalship should not be underestimated. His defeat of Harold Hardraada – widely reputed to be the most formidable warrior of the day – and his rapid marches to and from the North show his capability and resolution. Harold's ability to summon the fyrd on at least three separate occasions in 1066 suggests that England possessed a sophisticated and efficient system of military recruitment and that his authority was widely respected. Nor is the apparent shortage of English archers at Hastings decisive proof that the Saxon army was out of date. Some scholars maintain that Harold used archers at Stamford Bridge but, because they were foot soldiers, he was unable to bring them south in time to confront William. However one judges the armies, the fact is that the Battle of Hastings lasted for an unusually long time and its result was in doubt until quite late in the day. This suggests that the opposing armies were well matched.

## THE AFTERMATH OF THE BATTLE

William had defeated and killed the king of England but he had not yet won the kingdom, nor even the crown. He waited for a few days near Hastings, expecting a delegation from the English nobility to surrender to him. The fact that they did not shows how little support there was among the English for his claim to the throne. William marched on Dover, which surrendered to him without resistance. He ordered the fortifications of Dover to be improved, prudently securing his line of retreat should it prove necessary. While at Dover, his army was ravaged by an outbreak of dysentery. Leaving the sick, William moved on to Canterbury, which also submitted without a fight. William himself then became ill and was forced to spend about a month in Kent. In London, the English nobility began to rally around Edgar Atheling, the surviving member of the royal dynasty that had ruled England since the ninth century. Although there is no evidence that Edgar was crowned, he clearly enjoyed the support of the citizens of London and a number of potentially powerful English lords, including the archbishops of Canterbury and York and the northern earls, Edwin and Morcar. As William resumed his progress and advanced on London, the city began to take up arms against him.

There was a skirmish outside the city, in which William's troops burned Southwark. However, London Bridge was too strongly defended for a direct assault on the city itself and William chose to isolate the capital instead. His army skirted London to the west, devastating the countryside as it went and he crossed the Thames at Wallingford where he received the submission of the archbishop of Canterbury. When he reached Berkhamsted in Hertfordshire, the northern earls, the archbishop

*Alan of Brittany, nephew of William, swearing allegiance to the king, from a fifteenth-century manuscript*

BRITISH LIBRARY/FAUST.B.VII.7v

of York and Edgar Atheling submitted to him. Doubtless cowed by William's power and the ruthlessness of his march round London, they also lacked the troops to mount an effective challenge to the Normans.

## WILLIAM'S CORONATION

Having received the submission of his chief enemies, William entered the capital. Despite the surrender of the political leadership at Berkhamsted, there is evidence that he encountered resistance in London and he immediately began building castles in and around the city to secure his hold on the capital (one of these was the Tower of London). He also arranged for his coronation to occur in Westminster, not in the City. This had symbolic importance as well, since Westminster Abbey had been built by Edward the Confessor and William was underlining his claim to be Edward's true heir.

William was crowned on Christmas Day 1066. The occasion was marred by an unfortunate event. The shouts of acclamation for the new king were misinterpreted by William's soldiers guarding the abbey. They thought that a riot was starting and responded by setting fire to the neighbouring houses. William of Poitiers later recalled:

*As the fire spread rapidly, the people in the church were thrown into confusion... Though they were terrified, they managed to carry on and complete the consecration of the king who was trembling violently.*

William's reign had begun inauspiciously.

## THE CONQUEST OF ENGLAND

It was probably not until 1075 that William could feel secure on his throne. There were rebellions against him every year until 1070. Harold's family were active in provoking rebellion in the West Country in 1068 and 1069, assisted by support from Ireland. There were also risings in Kent, East Anglia and the Welsh Marches. The most serious threat occurred in 1069 when a hostile coalition of the northern earls and Edgar Atheling was supported by the king of Denmark, Cnut's nephew, and Malcolm, the king of Scotland. William suppressed these rebellions and on occasion showed extreme ruthlessness in his retribution. The suppression

of the northern rising was followed in the winter of 1069–70 by a period known as 'the harrying of the North'. Orderic Vitalis, writing in Normandy in the first half of the twelfth century, condemned William's military expedition to the North in his *Ecclesiastical History*, saying:

*In consequence, so serious a scarcity was felt in England and so terrible a famine fell upon the humble and defenceless populace that more than 100,000 Christian folk of both sexes, young and old alike, perished of hunger. My narrative has frequently had occasion to praise William, but for this act which condemned the innocent and guilty alike to die by slow starvation I cannot commend him...I am so moved to pity that I would rather*

*lament the griefs and sufferings of the wretched people than make a vain attempt to flatter the perpetrator of such infamy.*

Within a few years of the Battle of Hastings, the Anglo-Saxon aristocracy had been almost totally replaced by Norman landlords. As many as 4,000 Anglo-Saxon nobles lost their lands to a group of fewer than 200 Norman barons. The new élite retained control of England by building castles at strategic points. There were few castles in England before 1066; by the turn of the century there were at least eighty-four. Gradually England succumbed to its new ruling class, who brought with them a new language and culture. This was to have a profound impact on English literature, music and church architecture as well as on politics and society.

*The Tower of London, which was built by William to secure his hold on the city*

*The Domesday Book, which was commissioned by William as a survey of his new kingdom. It was an astonishing undertaking and includes details of land tenure across the country*

# THE HISTORY OF BATTLE ABBEY

~ TRADITIONALLY, BATTLE ABBEY WAS SAID TO HAVE BEEN FOUNDED TO FULFIL A VOW MADE BY DUKE WILLIAM BEFORE THE BATTLE. ~

*Reconstruction drawing of part of the monks' common room as it might have appeared in the fifteenth century, by Peter Urmston*

*The seal of Battle Abbey depicting the west front of the abbey church*

*Right: Monks giving alms to the poor, from a fourteenth-century manuscript*

*Opposite: An aerial view of Battle Abbey from the south-east. Beyond lies the town, which owes its origin and medieval prosperity to the abbey*

William promised to establish a monastery free of episcopal control if God granted him victory. This pleasing story first appears in a forged charter of 1154, produced by the monks as part of their struggle to maintain exemption from the jurisdiction of the bishop of Chichester in whose diocese the abbey lay. More prosaically, William's vow was probably made about 1070. That year, the papal authorities imposed heavy penalties on the Normans for the bloodshed of the conquest of England. An abbey founded here as an act of penance by the king would not only please his followers and honour the dead of the battle, but it would also help populate a comparatively empty stretch of country which had only recently shown itself to be a good invasion route. In naming it Battle Abbey, the new Norman regime demonstrated its self-confidence, not to say arrogance.

BRITISH LIBRARY ROY.16.6.VI

28

## BUILDING THE ABBEY

Four monks from the Benedictine abbey of Marmoutier on the Loire came to form the nucleus of the new community. William apparently intended the abbey to have sixty monks initially and ultimately to be capable of supporting 140. There is no reason to doubt the story that William wished the high altar of the church to be placed where Harold had been killed, nor that the monks were appalled when they saw the site. To place a monastery on this narrow ridge was to incur extra building costs, involving the monks in extensive terracing and the construction of massive undercrofts. More importantly, the hilltop lacked a water supply.

*Monks conducting a burial, from a fourteenth-century* Book of Hours

Not surprisingly, construction began on a more favourable location to the west, but when William heard this, he ordered the monks back to the hilltop. As the monks had no endowments, the king's treasury funded all building costs and by 1076 the eastern arm of the abbey church was sufficiently advanced to allow it to be consecrated.

Battle Abbey followed normal monastic planning, with the monks' quarters laid out round a cloister on the south side of the abbey church. West of the cloister was the outer court, while to the east were the secluded and peaceful buildings of the infirmary. Surrounding the complex was a precinct wall, dominated by the gatehouse, which linked the outer court to the town of Battle.

In February 1094 the completed abbey church was consecrated in the presence of William II, the Archbishop of Canterbury and seven bishops. William the Conqueror had bequeathed to the community on his death his royal cloak, a collection of relics and a portable altar used during his military campaigns. Of far greater practical importance, however, were his gifts of land to Battle Abbey. These had been so generous that it was then the fifteenth wealthiest

religious house in England. The most remarkable gift was his granting of the 'leuga' to the monks. This was all the land within a league, or one and a half miles, of the high altar of the abbey church. Within this area the abbey had widespread immunity from secular authorities, and the abbot enjoyed supreme jurisdiction over land and men. Although largely undeveloped, careful management of the land, especially by Abbot Ralph, quadrupled its value between 1086 and 1115.

*Right: Fragment of an ivory Tau cross, originally the upper terminal of an ecclesiastical staff, dating from the early twelfth century*

## THE MONKS' DIET

Surviving cellarers' accounts show that in the later medieval period the monks enjoyed a varied fare. Outside fast periods they were allowed meat for three main meals each week and fish or eggs at the other four. Beef, mutton and pork were consumed in large quantities, while the staple fish was herring, pickled, salted and dried. Cod and mackerel were also consumed in significant amounts, while oysters and mussels were introduced in the fifteenth century. Beer was drunk, and wines were also a regular feature of the monks' diet, reflecting the abbey's proximity to Winchelsea importers.

*A reconstruction drawing of monks in the common room, by Peter Urmston*

## THE ABBEY IN ITS HEYDAY

Contemporary documents tell us a great deal about the abbey's life, but they tend to record the unusual: disputes with bishops, petitions to the king, encroachments on abbey lands and, in the fourteenth century, upsets caused by French raids on the coast. In the background, forming the linking thread, was the ordered routine of the daily life of the monks. If such a routine has less appeal today, it should be remembered that for many it gave security in an often troubled and violent world. Moreover, the establishment of a monastery at Battle had important economic repercussions on what was then a sparsely populated and remote area. Traders, especially craftsmen and producers of luxury items such as silversmiths, depended heavily on the abbey's patronage.

Although the monks lived sheltered lives centred on church and cloister, they needed servants and estate workers to provide food, fuel and clothing and to look after their lands and buildings. West of the church and cloister, but inside the precinct wall, lay the outer court with its barns, storehouses and workshops – the link, as it were, between monastic and secular worlds. To cater for this community, the town of Battle was established north of the abbey.

In its first 150 years, one of the abbey's most intractable problems was how to maintain its freedom from episcopal control. This was a rare prize for an abbey and one not to be relinquished lightly. Because of its royal foundation, Battle Abbey claimed such a right and it had no difficulty in upholding it during the lifetimes of William the Conqueror and his son. The problem was how to sustain the claim in the long term, when later monarchs did not have the same personal interest in the abbey, and the abbey lacked a royal charter specifically stating this right. Successive Bishops of Chichester disputed the claim, and it was not until 1235 that an amicable compromise was reached.

Much of the abbey's energies in the thirteenth century were concentrated on renewing most of the buildings around the cloister and then extending the abbey church.

*The deed of surrender of the abbey in 1538, signed by the abbot and eighteen monks*

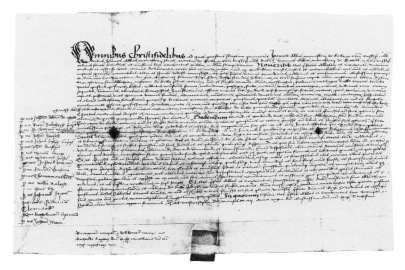

## THE LIVES OF THE MONKS

Monks at Battle Abbey lived an ordered life, following the rules of St Benedict and the guidance of their abbots. Their 'horarium' or daily timetable was governed by the seasons with their different festivals and fast days. Typically, the first service, very early in the day, was Nocturns, to be followed by Matins around dawn. There was a third service before the monks went to the cloister for a period of reading, perhaps lasting a couple of hours. Around 9 o'clock they returned to the dormitory, washed, put on their day shoes and returned to the church for the services of Tierce and Mass. After Mass, the monks adjourned to the chapter house for the daily reading of a chapter of the Benedictine Rule, to learn of any special duties and to go through the practical business of the community. Afterwards, the monks devoted themselves to reading or work – perhaps copying some of the manuscripts in the scriptorium before returning to the church for the services of Sext, High Mass and None at noon. About 2 o'clock they went to the dining hall for the only substantial meal of the day which was followed by more work and reading. Just before sunset they returned to the church for Vespers and then went to the dining hall for a drink. Compline was the last service of the day, finishing about 7 o'clock, after which the monks retired to the dormitory.

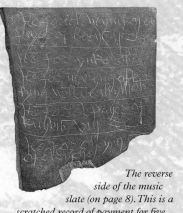

*The reverse side of the music slate (on page 8). This is a scratched record of payment for five items, including ink and the cost of repairing a pair of boots*

## TROUBLED TIMES

During the Hundred Years' War with France in the fourteenth century, the abbey's life was to be disturbed in a way very different from the legal squabbles with the bishops of Chichester. From the 1330s almost to the end of the century, the abbots were to be the main organisers of defence against French raids on the coast between Romney Marsh and the Pevensey Levels. Winchelsea, then an important wine port and embarkation point for troops crossing to France, was the chief target and it was here in the summer of 1377 that Abbot Hamo gained enduring fame when he led local forces and routed a French raid. As attacks worsened, the abbey almoner was kept busy providing food and clothing for poor refugees fleeing from the coastal communities. Tangible evidence of these unsettled times can be seen today in the great fortified gatehouse rebuilt as a stronghold in 1338, and in the adjacent length of precinct wall.

In the midst of these troubles, the abbey did not escape the Black Death which probably halved the population of the town and reduced the number of monks and novices from fifty-two in 1347 to thirty-four in 1352. Their numbers never recovered and they were later to drop to around twenty-five. Plague and French raids also contributed to a drop in the abbey's income and careful management was needed to avoid serious debt. In spite of these vicissitudes, the community remained vigorous, and in the fifteenth century parts of the cloister were again rebuilt and extensive alterations were made to the abbot's lodgings in the west range.

The abbey's lands enabled it to be largely self-sufficient for food, as well as providing recreation for the community. The manor of Alciston on the Sussex Downs was a favourite resort of the abbots; they also enjoyed riding and hawking in the marshes of the Pevensey Levels near their manor of Barnhorn. Small groups of monks were also sent here to rest while others went to the almoner's house at Maxfield near Winchelsea. Nearer to home, the monks took exercise just north-east of the town of Battle in the Little Park; the Great Park, south of the abbey, lay over much of the old site of the Battle of Hastings.

In 1529 John Hamond was elected abbot amidst growing signs that monastic life was under serious threat from the state. In the summer of 1535, Thomas Cromwell, Henry VIII's chief minister, sent his notorious official, Richard Layton, to inspect the abbey. He described Hamond in a now-famous phrase as 'the veriest hayne, beetle and buserde and the arentest chorle that ever I see' ('the lowest clod, stupidest numbskull, and the most out-and-out bumpkin I ever met'). By the spring of 1538 only Robertsbridge and Battle Abbeys remained in Sussex. The former surrendered on 16 April, followed by Battle on 27 May when Hamond and eighteen monks left the buildings. Battle had an income of £880 in 1535 making it one of the more prosperous Benedictine houses and a rich prize for the king's treasury. Abbot Hamond was given the substantial pension of £100 a year and moved to a house on the opposite side of Battle High Street, where he died in 1546.

# THE DISSOLUTION OF THE MONASTERIES

When Henry VIII became supreme head of the Church in England in 1534, it marked his formal break with Rome. This originated in the Pope's refusal to annul Henry's marriage to Catherine of Aragon who was unable to produce a male heir for Henry. As head of the Church, Henry continued work first begun by Cardinal Wolsey in the 1520s to reform lax religious practices. In 1536, the Act of Suppression prompted the closure of smaller monasteries with an income of less than £200 a year. Monks and nuns from these houses were transferred to the larger communities where religion was more strictly observed. Lands from the closed monasteries were either added to the royal estates or were sold to raise revenue. In 1538, faced with the need to raise more money to meet the threat of war with the Catholic powers of Europe, and conscious that there was little public sympathy for monks and nuns, Henry VIII ordered the suppression of the remaining large monasteries and the confiscation of their lands, a process which was completed by 1540.

PUBLIC RECORD OFFICE

*Henry VIII, as depicted in the* Valor Ecclesiasticus, *Cromwell's survey of church property of 1535*

## LATER HISTORY

In August 1538 Battle Abbey and a substantial proportion of its lands were given by Henry VIII to his friend and Master of the Horse, Sir Anthony Browne. He demolished the church, chapter house and part of the cloister and took over the west range as his residence, in effect turning it into a country house. Reputedly named guardian of Prince Edward and Princess Elizabeth, he rebuilt the monastic guest house as a possible royal residence, but in the event neither of the children ever came to Battle. Sir Anthony did well from the Dissolution, at one time owning Bayham and Waverley Abbeys, Easebourne Priory and St Mary Overy Nunnery in London. In 1542 he inherited Cowdray House from his half-brother the earl of Southampton. He died in 1548 and was buried in Battle church, where his effigy and that of his first wife recline in splendour on a magnificent tomb chest. Sir Anthony's son was created first viscount Montague. The estate continued to be owned by his family until the sixth viscount sold it in 1715 to Sir Thomas Webster.

In the 1680s, the monastic kitchen had been demolished, while in the eighteenth century Sir Whistler Webster destroyed the guest range built by Sir Anthony Browne. In 1752 Horace Walpole was moved to write that 'the grounds, and what has been the park, lie in a vile condition'. However, the fifth baronet, Sir Geoffrey Vassall Webster, spent considerable sums on the west range in the late eighteenth and early nineteenth centuries, and he also excavated the crypt chapels of the abbey church. Perhaps the most enthusiastic owners were the Duke and Duchess of Cleveland, who lived in the abbey between 1857 and 1901. In 1858 they employed the architect Henry Clutton to build a library at the south-west end of the west range and they also spent modest

*The tomb of Sir Anthony Browne and his wife, Alice, in Battle parish church. Sir Anthony died in 1548, ten years after being given the Battle Abbey estate by Henry VIII*

*The abbot's range from the west in 1783. The two octagonal towers in the right foreground are all that remain of Sir Anthony Browne's remodelling of the guest range*

*The former medieval undercroft below the abbot's great chamber. This view shows it in use as a drawing room by the Duchess of Cleveland in around 1900*

*Battle Abbey and the Battle of Hastings have long attracted visitors, as is shown in this photograph of French tourists, taken some seventy years ago*

sums repairing the abbey ruins. After the First World War the west range was leased to a school who still occupy it. It was extensively damaged by fire on 31 January 1931 but was carefully restored under the direction of the architect and antiquary, Sir Harold Brakespear. Distantly echoing the events of 1066, Battle Abbey was occupied in the Second World War by British and Canadian troops preparing for the invasion of Normandy in 1944. This time, however, the forces crossing the Channel to William the Conqueror's former lands were an army of liberation not conquest. The estate remained in the Websters' possession until it was acquired for the nation in 1976.

# A LUCKY ESCAPE

Aᴸᵀᴴᴼᵁᴳᴴ the gatehouse was built with defence in mind, it was never actually attacked by French raiders and nor was the abbey. Some 600 years later, the gatehouse had a fortunate escape when the abbey was occupied by the British army during part of the Second World War. On 2 February 1943 a German aircraft bombed Battle High Street. One bomb hit the ground, skidded through the gatehouse past a sentry, knocking away his rifle before damaging the lower part of the western gate and the adjacent pier and hitting the porter's doorway and the western pedestrian arch. It then broke up

on the lawn without exploding. It is possible to trace the path of this bomb by the carefully renewed stonework. The sentry's comments are not recorded!

*The abbey and town had a narrow escape during the Second World War, when a bomb nearly hit the gatehouse. Locals are shown here inspecting the damage*

*Battle Abbey gatehouse in the 1920s*

*Battle Abbey School in the 1950s*

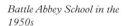

# FURTHER READING

R. Allen Brown, *The Normans and the Norman Conquest*, London, 1969

R. Allen Brown, 'The Battle of Hastings', in *Proceedings of the Battle Conference 1980*, edited by R. Allen Brown, Woodbridge, 1981

H. Brakespear, 'The Abbot's House at Battle', *Archaeologia*, LXXXIII, 1933, pp.139–66

R. Gilyard-Beer, *Abbeys*, London, 1958

B. Golding, *Conquest and Colonisation: The Normans in Britain, 1066–1100*, Houndmills, 1994

J. N. Hare, 'The Buildings of Battle Abbey', in *Proceedings of the Battle Conference 1980*, edited by R. Allen Brown, Woodbridge, 1981

J. N. Hare, *Battle Abbey: The Eastern Range and the Excavations of 1978–80*, London, 1985

R. Holmes, *War Walks 2: From the Battle of Hastings to the Blitz*, London, 1997

H. R. Loyn, *Anglo-Saxon England and the Norman Conquest*, London and New York, 1991

T. McAleavy, *Life in a Medieval Abbey*, London, 1996

S. Morillo ed., *The Battle of Hastings*, Woodbridge, 1996

E. Searle, *Lordship and Community: Battle Abbey and its Banlieu 1066–1538*, Pontifical Institute of Medieval Studies, Toronto, 1974

E. Searle, *The Chronicle of Battle Abbey*, Oxford, 1980

E. Searle and B. Ross, *Accounts of the Cellarers of Battle Abbey 1275–1513*, Sydney, 1967

I. W. Walker, *Harold: The Last Anglo-Saxon King*, Thrupp, 1997

*One of the earliest-known drawings of the abbey, dating to around 1700. The buttressed building in the foreground is the former guest range, as rebuilt by Sir Anthony Browne*

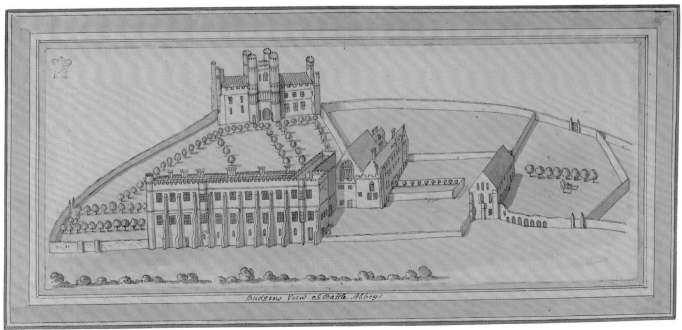

Budgens View of Battle Abbey